Codependent
Shackles...Broken!

Codependent Shackles...Broken!

Linda Valentine

Writers Club Press
San Jose New York Lincoln Shanghai

Codependent Shackles...Broken!

Writers Club Press
an imprint of iUniverse.com, Inc.

For information address:
iUniverse.com, Inc.
5220 S 16th, Ste. 200
Lincoln, NE 68512
www.iuniverse.com

ISBN: 0-595-16109-X

Printed in the United States of America

Contents

—King James
Isaiah 61:1

"The Spirit of the Lord God is upon me;
because the Lord hath anointed me to
preach good tidings unto the meek; he
hath sent me to bind up the brokenhearted,
to proclaim liberty to the captives,
and the opening of the prison to
them that are bound"

Jesus-

—King James
Luke 4:18

"The Spirit of the Lord is upon me, because he hath anointed me to preach the gospel to the poor; he hath sent me to heal the brokenhearted, to preach deliverance to the captives, and recovering of sight to the blind, to set at liberty them that are bruised,"

Jesus

*"All my pain will be worthwhile,
if I can help someone, somewhere,
break free from the shackles of....
Codependency."*

Dear Father in Heaven...

You have taught me all about the danger of depending on others for my happiness, and you have taught me well...

For this knowledge, I thank you...

You have allowed these things to happen to me that I might see and learn from them.

Now I write them down that others may learn, also, from my hardships.

I ask that you grant to all who read this book the understanding of your amazing love and your desire to set them free. I ask that each one will experience the renewing of life through Jesus, your Son.

Please grant to them, my Lord, the knowledge of your power and your degree of protection for your own.

For it's all in the Name of Jesus I ask—

"What Is Codependency?"

I have been inspired to write this book to help bring you into the awareness of your state of Codependency and to offer you a way of recovery from it. I want to help you understand that you do not have to stay in bondage.

Codependency has a simple yet complex meaning. Simple to those who have experienced the abuse of it—complex to those who are still in chains from it. Simple to those who are now in recovery to find the depths of damages of codependency, complex to those who refuse to try and recover. My definition of codependency is, "to be partially or totally dependent on another person or habit for happiness and existence."

Codependency is received very easily. It comes through various channels. The most common channel it arrives by is loving others too much. It comes unexpected and unaware. Codependency is a learned trait, which carries through the generations because of the same reason. We could have watched our grandmothers act as servants to our grandfathers by taking them a glass of water out of verbal demand and possibly never heard our grandfathers say thank you or even recognition of gratitude. We possibly never watched our grandfathers serve our grandmothers so this instantly painted a servant picture in our mind. We could have watched our dads ridicule our mothers openly in front of others to control and cause our mothers to fear. We possibly never heard our mothers defend themselves and this gave us the weaker image. Yet, our grandmothers and mothers could have continued being slaves and caring more for others than for themselves. Codependents have traits we can recognize easily when we start our recovery. We, too, were the same way once—but now we are on a brand new path learning new things every day about ourselves and others. Listed below are the most common traits I found as a codependent and the hardest I am finding to defeat in my recovery.

1) I allowed myself to be controlled by others,
2) I had low self-esteem,
3) I tried to fix everything wrong,
4) I was a people-pleaser,
5) I planned my escapes when the pain became unbearable,
6) I was afraid,
7) I would worry over things beyond my control.

My codependency operated by the spirit of fear-satan's favorite tool.

1) I would fear if I did not allow others to tell me what to do, they will be angry with me and I was afraid of confrontations.
2) I would fear I was not as good as the next person for one reason or another so that convinced me I was nobody.
3) I feared for others safety or sanity so much that I tried to fix their problems. Before recovery, I was not programmed to understand that I had no control over certain situations. I would fear others would be unhappy if I did not do what they had commanded me to.
4) I had the choice to either flee or fight. I was afraid to fight and I was afraid to flee. Because I did neither, I went into depression, another way of escape.
5) I would fear the bad and overlook the good. I would feel I was not worthy of good things to happen to me.
6) I was convinced I was nothing and that God did not love me enough to give me His best. I was convinced that he loved others more than me so therefore; others were always more blessed than I. A teaching from the past had somehow taught me that what was written was not necessarily the way it was today...and I believed them. I did not challenge myself to believe God's Word to be 100% true in every aspect until I was forced to believe Him for help.

As I stated earlier, codependency is a learned state of mind, so naturally, it will be a learned recovery. It will be a daily recovery because it was programmed into the memory banks of our mind daily. The road is simple...but long and never-ending. The path is set when you realize something is wrong because you are depending too much on another person for your happiness.

Reality may begin as simply as a disagreement with the one you love. For example, the disagreement could be over what kind of ice cream to order when you are dining out. The disagreement possibly gets heated to argument stage, then, it becomes filled with words of anger and hate. It reaches the point of total destruction of the relationship. If this happens, and your happiness within yourself becomes so threatened that you are miserable at the thought of life without him or her—you have a problem. If losing someone you love threatens your happiness to the point of self-destruction you have a problem.

It is perfectly normal to love someone with all your heart, however; you must be able to determine where the line is drawn in loving too much. You must be happy within yourself at all times. The only way to be totally happy is through Jesus Christ. Jesus can fill your heart with true love if you will totally submit your entire body, soul, and spirit to Him. You will find yourself falling in love with Jesus and you will want to become totally dependent on Him for everything that touches you.

I want to help you to understand that true happiness comes from within yourself. Happiness cannot depend on the fact of whether someone loves you or not. Don't wait until you are forced to live within yourself to find out who you really are.

When you realize you do have a problem within yourself, there are a couple of decisions you must make.

Your 1ˢᵗ decision is:

To give your heart and life to Jesus and expect Him to help you because—

You will not be able to make it by yourself!

The 2ⁿᵈ decision is:

*To Determine in your heart and mind that your life will change because now you **are** totally dependent on Him. He is God and He **never** fails!*

*Recovery from Codependency is daily-It requires walking with Jesus daily expecting Him to deliver you from **all** your trouble as He stated in His Word.*

As we walk with God daily-totally dependent on Him and no one else, we will experience the real meaning of life...and we will begin to appreciate the simple gifts of life. We will truly experience real life through Jesus!

—Reference King James
Luke 9-23 And he said to them all, If any
man will come after me, let him deny
himself, and take up his cross
daily, and follow me.

Introduction

Codependency...was a new word for me in March of 1993 and I did not experience the meaning of the word until a traumatic truth was told to me, which shattered the privacy of my personal life. This truth sent my comfortable identity soaring into another world I did not know existed. I did not know this experience would change my life forever and lead me into a journey in which, I would never return.

*In this book, I will be telling you my experiences and my viewpoints on **Codependency**. I will tell you of its cruelty and how I was almost destroyed by it. I will share with you how I was healed!*

*I will be sharing with you my personal thoughts on **Codependency** created from relationships. I will share with you why I feel this mental dependency is so destructive. Until I was healed, I was a victim of mental abuse. Psychological humiliation and isolation have been cited by abused victims as being their worst experiences. (Reference YWCA Family Violence Program). My life, before I was healed, testifies of this fact.*

If this codependent awareness comes to you, you may discover someone you trusted your life to has betrayed you. You may discover someone you gave every intimate detail of yourself to, has humiliated you. You may find someone you believed in has denied you. You may find that you even surrendered your God-given identity to this person. You may realize you have sacrificed your own dreams and have fallen so deeply into codependency that you now worship this person unaware.

We somehow expected them to give the same of themselves to us; after all, that was the oath they made on our wedding day. We believed in that person and the fact we would never be betrayed. Then one dreaded day, after months, or even years of relationship and total sacrifice we are brought to the truth that we were not as special to them as we thought.

At this point, we feel as though we have wasted our life! We feel we **have no life!** *We have reached a place where nothing seems to make any sense! We are now in a place where nothing matters! We feel we have no hope! For some of us, suicidal thoughts are being entertained, for the pain we feel is just too great to bear. This is the time we must choose to live! We must choose to live again but this time...wiser!*

It is true that hurt, grief, sadness, and depression are present, but I am here to offer help to you!

Let me introduce you to Jesus. He is my best friend; His name is Wonderful, Counselor, Almighty God, and Prince of Peace. He will give you the strength you need to make it. He will comfort you when all others are gone. He will take your pain away. Jesus will never leave you nor forsake you. Jesus will always be there for you.

I know...He did it for me and He will do it for you!

Welcome!
To Recovery from Codependency!

This is your chance to receive a
REAL Friend and have a brand new
Life!

Reference : King James
Hebrews 13:5 Let your conversation be without covetousness; and be content with such things as ye have: for he hath said, "I will never leave thee, nor forsake thee."

Chapter One

"Whipped and Beaten"

"WHIPPED AND BEATEN"

Growing up in a home of demanding structure and religious standards, I was taught from an early age the characteristics of what we now know as:

"Codependency"

I viewed my mother as the best, always taking care of my Dad with his every little command. As a child, I watched her as she continually humbled herself to please him in every way. Often times I heard her call him as he watched television to come for his shower. She would always call him when the water was the right temperature and when she had all his clothes placed so neatly on the counter. Such services rendered would qualify as a servant for a king.

My mother had four children and the demands were great. If you added my dad...she had five. This was not an option but her command to wait on him. My! How I admired that kind of love! Just the way I thought, to take care of a man; however, what I seemed to miss was the exchange of service given from my Dad to my Mom. Occasional gratitude would have been nice to hear. I do not remember, though, my Dad ever saying or doing any of those things for my Mom or his children. I don't remember many, "Thank You's" from my Dad to anyone for anything. **With all respect to these facts, this man is my Dad, and I love him in spite of his mentally abusive and controlling ways.** My Dad, along with many others, just did not realize the problem he really had with trying to control. My Dad never talked to me. If he did talk to me, he would be complaining or cursing. He always blamed my Mom or one of his children for his mistakes, or for another person's error.

Either way, we the children and my Mom, always caught the blame. At the time, it seemed all in place and no questions were ever asked why he did not return any expressions of love or gratitude.

My Mom never had the freedom to express her identity in the style of clothes she would wear. She did not shop for just the right look to match her identity—the freedom most women experience and take for granted. Mom did not ever display confidence in herself of how she looked or her ability to handle confrontations. Mom never defended herself or her children. She always felt she might hurt someone in something she would say. She would place the feelings of others in her life over the feelings of her children. The control from others was just too great!...and she felt helpless! She spent her life totally devoted to a controller, shackled by chains of codependency, and the saddest part never realizing it. I watched her carefully, and I loved her so much. It was natural for me to believe she handled everything in just the right way. She was a wonderful person!

When I was a child and as far back as I can remember, I was labeled with words of hate which created a tremendous inferiority complex in me. I was plagued with words that through time created chains of bondage by relatives. These people professed to love me—but fell a little short in showing love. These relatives professed to care about me but inwardly, I feel, had set goals to destroy me. It seemed they were determined to mark me with defeat at my early age!

Words such as, "Your hair is a mess, didn't you comb it before you left home?" I suppose they did not notice the perfection by which it was combed, the hair spray, and the coordinating ribbon my mother had placed in my hair. My clothes were sewn with love and every dress had coordinating apparel to wear with it. My shoes were shining and clean. When I wore new dresses, I was sure to hear, "Is that the best dress you have? Did your Mother really think those colors matched? She didn't do a very good job this time, did she?"

It seemed these statements would always come after wearing a new dress my mother had sewn for me. She was an excellent seamstress with natural talents to create. These words were spoken in so much hate and contempt they would penetrate my tender spirit each time I heard them. The laughter that followed only applauded the hate filled words that followed me for many years until I was in total bondage to them. I had been robbed of confidence...essential for a successful life.

Even as a child, I wondered how they could say these mean things to me when we were on our way to church. I remember running home and crying to my Mother because I had been so hurt. My eyes would swell from sobbing and I would feel so totally ashamed of myself.

Then with swollen eyes, Mom would send me back to my Grandmother's house so I would not miss the trip with them to church. She did not want the relatives to be upset because I did not go...after I had told them I would go. I would have to go to church with these people only to hear them laugh and call me names because I had cried. I remember seeing the hurt in my mother's eyes over this degrading situation. This is probably the most hurtful memory of all. My mother and dad always went to church, but I enjoyed going to church services with these relatives. The music was wonderful at their church and has always been my love.

I was attracted to the style they had, and the expressive perfumes caught my attention. They seemed to have wealth, but now, I realize there is more to life than wealth!

Another occasion of rejection would be when I would go to my grandmother's house after church. Every Sunday before we would go to church, Mama would have taken the time to cook a Sunday meal. We would always hurry to eat because we knew our cousins would be coming to our grandmother's house to visit and have Sunday lunch. We wanted to get there as soon as we could because we were so excited they were coming. We would run down the beaten trail to Grandma's house. The house would smell so good, and the squeaky wooden floor of her house announced to everyone that we were there. You could hear the aspirations come from the kitchen from the relatives in dread of our arrival. Entering the kitchen we could see the table set full of rich, tasty food. Pies of several kinds, more than one kind of meat, and so many different vegetables there was not enough room for the table to hold them all. I can see it all now...how these people would sit at the crowded table all hunched over their plates, greasy, apple red polished finger nails, red smeared lipsticks, a suit and tie protected by a dirty dish towel around the neck, while they enjoyed pork chops and mashed potatoes. When they saw me come through the door, they would all say almost in harmony, "Go on back home now, there is not enough for you your mama should have cooked for you. You can't have any go on back home." I remember them looking at me, and I wondered why we were hated so much. Most times I would drop my head and step backward, just as a little scolded puppy. Sometimes I would put my finger in my mouth for shame and embarrassment only to hear one of my aunts scold me for having no manners.

She would tell me to get my finger out of my mouth and to stop it, in a very cruel way! No matter what it took...these relatives would not stop until they got the reaction they wanted...and that was to persecute me to tears! This type of verbal abuse was every Sunday for sure and six other days of the week. It seemed the pain would never stop! My parents were not poor, but they were not wealthy either. Pork chops and mashed potatoes were rarely seen in the 50's in our neighborhood. I am sure you can imagine the hungry look that I gave, as it seemed we were begging crumbs from their table. Could they not spare a few morsels of food for their brother's children?

Another childhood memory I found stored in my mind on Shelf Number 7700, takes place in the summer. One of my cousins, spent the summer with my grandmother. At that time, she owned a country store. In that store, she had plenty of snacks, potato chips, cookies, ice-cold glass bottled beverages, everything a child would want on a hot scorching day.

My grandmother would call him at approximately 10:30 in the morning to see if he had awaken. She called to get his order for the day. "Do you want your Orange today or had you rather have a Cola? Do you want chocolate cupcakes? Or do you want chips? Well, why don't I just send all of it and you can choose what you want", she would say. "Is your cousin there? Well, tell her I don't have enough for her. I will send this by a neighbor so meet him when he comes to the mailbox. Just tell her to go on home and come back later. Be sure and wait for our neighbor! I love you..."she would say. Anxiously, we ran to meet the neighbor. In a sack, we would find all sorts of snacks. And...a six-pack of his favorite! This would be at about 10:00 in the morning, on a very hot day. "Sorry," he would say to me. "Grandma said you could not have any. She said for you to go home, now. She said maybe you could come back after I finish my breakfast. I will talk to you in awhile and maybe we will go play in the creek and catch some tadpoles," he would say.

I would leave again. Not truly understanding why he could not share with me, because we had been taught to share, but knowing I could not enjoy his snack for that day. I remember these days and it is a miracle I survived the constant abuse I received in my childhood. How could someone be so cruel to a child...their own grandchild and niece?

Did they despise my dad, their brother, so much that they vented their hatred on his children? Were they so envious of the love we had in our family that they tried to destroy us because of it? After years of being beaten with words of hate, mocked, and ridiculed constantly, I was convinced I was nobody, with no direction, to always be at the mercy of those who tormented. I was mentally abused and in the lowest state one could be.

I married at 17 years old and because I had been under the rule of a controller all my life, I found another to rule and reign over me. I really thought this was the way to live. I loved him so much and I tried to fix his every problem. It did not matter whether it was the amount of food I would put on his plate, or, if it was bringing him water in his favorite glass, I tried to keep him happy continually. I served him and I worshipped him. I felt if I gave my 100% of myself to my husband and to my marriage, I would not have any problems. This was a favorite teaching from my relatives. As a child, grabbing on to every word, I felt secure in that teaching and never doubted my marriage would go bad or troubled as some of the others. I had no way of knowing the pain I would have to experience to gain freedom in my life.

All my life, I had served someone with every kindness I could possibly give, and had not received anything in return. Because of all the mental abuse I had received in my childhood and even in my married life, I was now totally dependent on others for everything. I had been convinced that I was incapable of taking care of myself, I was convinced I did not have the knowledge to think for myself, I had been convinced that without others I would surely fail. I was soundly convinced I was the ugliest person living on planet earth. Not only did I have these feelings of being inferior, rejected, and zero self-esteem, I had become mentally chained to controllers.

Chapter Two

Alone and Adrift

ALONE & ADRIFT

I was sitting on my family's porch on this lazy, hazy afternoon listening to the buzz of a fishing boat while I soaked up the stillness of the lake. I was all alone and all was very still.

I began thinking how nice it would be to just float along the lake today. I listened to the muffled voices of the fishermen as they traveled across the still waters.

It was then I had a revelation about life...

It feels good sometimes just to relax and float; to take everything in stride, just as it would be to float along the lake today out of control drifting aimlessly about no motor...no disturbances...just to sleep in the peace.

But, to wander with no direction would suddenly become very frightening if there became a remote possibility we could not start the engine and come home...That is the way of life.

There is great peace in not being concerned about tomorrow, but we still want to know we can help in controlling our destiny.

Written by:

Mary Jones
my daughter, my Scientist
who refuses to be...

"Codependent"

Chapter Three

"Shipwrecked"

"SHIPWRECKED"

After struggling to hold to my sanity from my childhood, my heart was overjoyed because I had just found a place to worship in freedom in truth. When I attended these services, I would leave feeling full of glory and powerful in might. I did not feel I could be hurt by anyone ever again. I felt I had reached a point of true happiness. I had found my place to worship and that really helped me through the darkness that I did not know was before me. However, I was still very dependent on my husband and I allowed myself to be under his control. I did not realize I was still chained to his emotions.

Please remember, my thinking had not yet been re-programmed. Having been trained by generations of people before me I was blinded from knowing who I was, my enjoyments of life, or the person God had called me to be. Therefore, I was content in being someone's wife, a mother, a housekeeper, a farmer, a landscaper, whatever my husband needed me to do.

As I was busy cleaning one day, after my daughters had gone to school, I experienced a vision I shall never forget. A vision, a warning, a premonition...whatever you may define it as being, came very clear to me. This may sound dramatized to you but in all truthfulness, this actually happened!

My story begins!

I believe the rain, thunder, and lightening of the storm that morning was a shadow of events about to happen in the spiritual and displayed in that physical morning. The house was dark that morning because the storm, which began during the night, lingered on. I had only a lamp burning in my family room. I had started my laundry a few hours earlier and I was walking down the hall to continue my work. As I entered the long hallway that led to my laundry room, I suddenly stopped...and lapsed into a different realm of time!

The scene was probably the same as when Paul lived in the New Testament. Please remember Paul had been on board a ship during a raging storm. His ship had wrecked so badly that he had only a broken board by which to float to shore.

Reference-King James
Acts 27:44 And the rest, some on
boards, and some on broken pieces
of the ship. And so it came to pass,
that they escaped all safe to land.

In my vision, I saw myself floating on a broken board drifting on a dark, cold, sea. Our ship had just wrecked. No one was in sight...the air was very cold, the water was even colder, and I was all alone.

At that moment, I looked up and saw a large wooden stamp, which read,

"SHIPWRECKED"

coming down toward me. I felt it stamp across my forehead. The vision had been overwhelming! I could not imagine what this meant. For the next few minutes I was entranced trying to discern what this was all about. Soon after, I conveniently dismissed this vision from my mind. Perhaps I chose not to prepare for the storm soon to come in my life or, perhaps it was for someone else...I told myself.

It was approximately two weeks later when my husband and I had traveled into a nearby city to grocery shop. I could tell he was deeply troubled. When I ask him about his quietness, he just shrugged his shoulders and assured me everything was fine.

A few miles down the road, he started to remind me of how long we had been married. He reminded me he had always loved me and he loved me still. His words were so comforting because my husband had become my very best friend. Through the 25 years of our marriage, I had loved him dearly and had grown to depend upon him for every need in my life. No matter what..., he was my best friend.

I had even placed him as the priority in my life...even above Jesus! After a few minutes of silence, he told me his true feelings and how he had tried to fight the war within. He told me the times his love for me tempted failure. He told me of his thoughts of infidelity, and he told me these things because he wanted to free his mind from the guilt. He assured me he had never failed me and did remain faithful, but he just needed to clear his conscious of the thoughts. All the years we were married, he had convinced me he was faithful and I was all he ever wanted or needed. He assured me for years he never lied to me about anything. Part of my childhood and Christianity included being taught to trust. Now, all of a sudden, he was telling me everything opposite of what I had believed from the first day of our marriage. Had my marriage been based on a lie? Had this man ever loved me at all? Have I been a fool for all these years in believing in him? All these questions raced through my mind all at one time!

At first, I tried to dismiss the conversation by denying I heard it, but denial gave way to truth. As the truth started to penetrate my heart, I started to weep then...I started to fear. By the time we reached the supermarket, I was sobbing uncontrollably. The weeping continued for hours. Just to think of my husband even possibly loving another woman just broke my heart to pieces. I could not get control of the feelings. It seemed my entire world had been crushed. Suddenly, I did not even know this man next to me at all. Once again, I felt all alone and horribly afraid.

What was I going to do? I wondered...I have no one. I can't make it through my life without him. He doesn't love me anymore. If he said he did now, how could I believe him...He said he loved me then but he lied. What will I do? At that point, my mind overloaded!

It was then I was reminded of the vision...the scene had returned.

Shipwrecked...all alone.

The vision I had on that morning a few weeks ago was true prophesy and now it had manifest itself to me. When we returned home, I felt totally lifeless. Pain and disbelief had consumed my being.

I went into my bedroom to lie down for awhile hoping I would find all of this to be a bad dream or a troubled imagination. In my desperation and mental fatigue, I fell to the floor and collapsed into a fetal position. I faintly remember my last words in the struggle to hold to my sanity.

"Oh, God! Help Me! there has to be more to life than this, Please help me!"

When my family found me, they told me I was completely covered with a blanket. My body was cold and clammy and I seemed to have no life at all.

For weeks after, I felt nothing. No pain, no hurt...nothing. My body, my mind, my spirit was numb. As weeks gave way to months, I started to feel a strange feeling flow through my body. The numbness I had felt now, somehow, felt warm and healing. Occasionally I would think about those steps I made as a child...those steps I had made when I was baptized like Jesus...those steps I had made to worship in freedom and truth. I started reading my Bible again! I started earnestly praying again! With each day that went by, I felt stronger, and more courageous! I felt daringly new! The change was obviously not of my making! It was God who gave me the real reason to live. God gave me His Son brand new with a promise and blessed assurance that He would never leave me nor forsake me. The communication I once had with Jesus...was now alive!

After several months, I realized the night I collapsed...was the night the Holy Spirit performed His healing surgery on me. He removed the pain and dependency I had on others and reserved me exclusively for Himself.

He was there waiting for me,
in His Recovery Room...
at His Throne!

He is still present with me today! In everything I do, He is here! I started to feel alive again, new, and alive! I did not understand what the change was all about, but, I have been changed!

God gave me His Son to be my friend no matter what time of night, no matter where I travel while in this world...He gave me a promise that I would never be alone again!

My experience happened several years ago and Jesus is still my best friend. Jesus is the true love of my life. Jesus gives me Peace when trouble and confusion is all around. Still today, I feel daringly new!

Praise God! My childhood troubles are all past, I now have that essential confidence for success that only God can give...and He gave it to me!

Jesus is the song I sing! Jesus is happiness when all around me is sad! Jesus is my laughter and joy!

My codependent shackles were broken that night...and while I was in that collapsed state, the Holy Spirit recreated me. He discarded all the hurt and scar tissue others had placed on me and made me specifically for His own! All my pain is gone, memories no longer hurt but are there only...to help me and you to know...Jesus is alive and is able!

—Reference King James
Isaiah 53:5 But he was wounded for our transgressions, he was bruised for our iniquities: the chastisement of our peace was upon him; and with his stripes we are healed.

—Reference King James
Psalms 107:20 He sent his word, and healed them, and delivered them from their destructions.-

Chapter Four

"Letter From My Friend"

A LETTER FROM MY FRIEND

Sunday Morn.
6:00 A.M.

Dear Linda

I really enjoyed visiting with you on the phone last night, although I sometimes feel like I'm an interruption to the family life when I call.

I wish we had more time to visit; you are a special friend, a blessing from the Lord in my life. One of the few people in life I've ever "clicked" with.

I continue to pray for you and your family and there's hardly a day that goes by that you don't cross my mind.

Be encouraged in knowing God has the upper hand and final say in every walk of your life. Expect a "word" from him in the nighttime hours while you sleep. I believe He will minister to you that way about the next phase of the book.

You will find a poem attached to this letter. I thought you might use it in your book.

Expect a miracle!

I love you
Jan

SCENARIO OF A BATTERED WOMAN
Written by Jan Wheeler-June 1996

Yes, he hit me but he didn't mean to
It was over in a minute, for something I failed to do.
He really loves me, most of the time
I try to be good and walk a straight line
I'm hurting now, but tomorrow I'll heal
I'll be the best I can, even cook his favorite meal
I threw up my hands to try to protect my face
Oh God! Why can't I forget the pain, it won't erase.
I'm so frightened, but I can't let you know
I must try harder to please him, there's no where I can go
The hatred in his eyes, the blows that came down
Etched in my memory, even his frown
Oh! If I could just run and get out of this hell
But, I really do need him without him I'll fail
Makeup won't hide the bruises anymore
I'm so ashamed and my body is so sore
Tomorrow will be better, it really will
He'll hold me in his arms until I'm asleep and I'm still
It won't ever happen again, he has promised me
I want to believe him but I want to be free
I wish my family was happy and secure once more
He really didn't mean that I am a whore
The incident is over now and I'm really okay
I'll just stay awhile longer and try some other way
I thought I needed help but I don't...you know...
so thank you officers for your time, but now you can go...

Chapter Five

"Chained?"

"Chained?"
(Signs of the Abusive Personality)

Sometimes we as codependents subconsciously search for controllers for companions. We have been programmed to depend on them from childhood, previous marriages, or other relationships. Because of the dependency we have on these kinds of personalities, we selectively ignore the signs and facts which will tell us what we need to know.

It could be the codependent does not want to face the facts because if they do...they may have to give up this controller. I hope by now you have realized you can no longer hide from the possibility of having a codependent personality.

These are a few of the signs.

1. JEALOUSY:

At the beginning of a relationship, an abuser will always say that the jealousy is a sign of love. Jealousy has nothing to do with love. It is a sign of insecurity and possessiveness. The abuser will question the victim about who they talk to, accuse them of flirting, or be jealous of time spent with family, friends or children. As the jealousy progresses, the abuser may call frequently during the day or drop by unexpectedly. The abuser may refuse to let the victim work for fear of meeting someone else. The abuser may even show strange behaviors such as checking car mileage or asking friends to watch this person.

2. CONTROLLING BEHAVIOR:

At first, the abuser will say that this behavior is because he or she is concerned for the their safety, the need for the victim to use their time wisely, or the need to make good decision. The abuser will be angry if the victim is "late" coming back from the store or an appointment, the abuser will question closely about where the victim went or who they talked to.

As this behavior gets worse, the abuser may not let the victim make personal decisions about the house, clothing, going to church, the abuser may keep all the money or even make her ask permission to leave the house or room.

3. QUICK INVOLVEMENT:

Statistics say many battered women dated or knew their abuser for less than six months before they were engaged or living together. He comes on like a whirlwind claiming" love at first sight", and he will tell the woman flattering things such as;

"You're the only person I could ever talk to", "I've never felt loved like this by anyone". The abuser needs someone desperately, and will pressure the victim to commit to him.

4. UNREALISTIC EXPECTATIONS:

The abuser is very dependent on the spouse for all needs. He or she expects a perfect spouse, mother or dad, lover, friend. The abuser will say things like "if you love me, I'm all you need you're all I need."

The victim is supposed to take care of everything emotionally and in the home.

5. ISOLATION:

The abuser tries to cut the victim off from all resources. If the victim has friends, he or she is a whore or homosexual, if the victim is close to family; their are "tied to the apron strings".

The abuser accuses people who support the victim of "causing trouble", the abuser may want to live in the country without a phone, he or she may not allow the use of a car, or may try to keep the victim from working or going to school.

6. BLAMES OTHERS FOR THE PROBLEMS:

If the abuser is chronically unemployed, someone is always doing them wrong, out to get him. He may make mistakes and then blame the woman for upsetting him and keeping him from concentrating or doing his job. He or she will tell the victim they are at fault for almost anything that goes wrong.

7. BLAMES OTHERS FOR THE FEELINGS:

The abuser may tell the victim, "You make me mad", "You're hurting me by not doing what I ask," "I can't help being angry". He or she really makes the decision about what they think and feel, but will use feelings to manipulate the victim. Harder to catch are the claims that "you make me happy", "you control how I feel".

8. HYPERSENSITIVITY:

The abuser is easily insulted, he or she claims his feelings are "hurt": when they are really very mad, or they take the slightest set backs as personal attacks. The abuser will "rant and rave" about the injustice of things that have happened to them—things that are really just part of living like having to work overtime, getting a traffic ticket, being asked to help with chores.

9. CRUELTY TO ANIMALS OR CHILDREN:

The abuser may punish animals brutally or is insensitive to their pain or suffering. He or she may expect children to be capable of doing things far beyond their ability (whips a two year old for wetting their diaper) or the abuser may tease children or young brothers and sisters until they cry.

(Statistics show Sixty percent of abusers who beat the women they are with also beat their children).

The abuser may not want children to eat at the table or expect them to keep to their room all evening while he or she is home.

10. PLAYFUL USE OF FORCE IN SEX:

This abuser may like to throw one down and hold them down during, sex, the abuser may want to act out fantasies during sex where the victim is helpless. The abuser lets the victim know that the idea of "rape" excites them. One may show little concern about whether the victim wants to have sex and use sulking or anger to manipulate into compliance. The abuser may start having sex with the victim while they are sleeping, or demand sex when one is ill or tired.

11. VERBAL ABUSE:

In addition to saying things that are meant to be cruel and hurtful, this can be seen by the abuser degrading the victim, cursing, running down any accomplishments. The abuser will say the victim is stupid and unable to function without them. This may involve waking the victim up to verbally abuse or not letting one go to sleep.

12. RIGID SEX ROLES:

The abuser expects the victim to serve him; will say they must stay at home, that they must obey them in all things even things that are criminal in nature. The abuser will see the victim as inferior, more stupid, unable to be a whole person without a relationship.

13. DR. JEKYLL AND MR. HYDE:

Many victims are confused by their abuser's sudden "changes in mood." They will describe that one minute they are nice and the next minute he or she explodes, or, one minute happy and the next minute sad. This does not indicate some special "mental problem" or that "he's crazy". Explosiveness and mood swings are typical of abusers who beat their partners, and these behaviors are related to other characteristics such as hypersensitivity.

14. THREATS OF VIOLENCE:

This would include any threat of physical force meant to control the victim. "I'll slap your mouth off", "I'll kill you", and "I'll break your neck". Most abusers do not threaten their mates, but an abuser will try to excuse this behavior by saying "everybody talks like that".

15. BREAKING OR STRIKING OBJECTS:

This behavior is used as a punishment when breaking loved possessions, but is mostly used to terrorize the victim into submission. The abuser may beat on tables with his fist, throw objects around or near the victim. Again, this is a very remarkable behavior; only very immature people beat on objects in the presence of other people in order to threaten them.

16. ANY FORCE DURING AN ARGUMENT:

This may involve an abuser holding a victim down, physically restraining her from leaving the room, any pushing or moving. The abuser may hold the victim against a wall and say "you're going to listen to me".

*(Reference YWCA Family Violence Program-pamphlet.
YWCA of Northwest LA)*

If any of these facts sound familiar to you, I challenge you to do something about it. You deserve a better life and more wonderful person than what you have now.

Jesus paid an awful price for our freedom and He did not intend for any of us to live in bondage to another individual.

Maybe it is time for you to ask yourself—

"Am I chained?"

Chapter Six

Levels of Sinkage

LEVELS OF SINKAGE

There are different levels or degrees of injury which result in being chained from an abusive relationship. The injury of one person may not be as devastating as another. The different levels possibly come from the underlying reason for the abuse and therefore may be more difficult to break than others. There are many reasons why women find it diffi-cult to leave a violent or abusive relationship:

1. HOPE—

Many victims love their partner and hope things will change. They recall the good parts of the relationship and wish they would return. The violent person often reinforces this by treating the victim very well during reconciliation following a violent episode. Many women want to believe in the promises and desirable behavior they see when their partner attempts to "make up".

2. FEAR—

Many times the violent person threatens to hurt the victim or others if she leaves the relationship. This includes threats of harm to her prop-erty or psychological harm, such as telling others damaging informa-tion. The victim often believes these threats because they have already seen that their partner is capable of violence.

3. SHAME

Victims often are reluctant to admit that their partner has abused them. Younger people may feel that if parents know that they have been abused, their freedom may be curtailed by the parent's attempts to protect them.

4. SOCIAL PRESSURE

In many social groups, it is expected that victims will have "boy or girl friends, dates, or partners". Sometimes it appears preferable to continue a bad relationship rather than give up the social status or sense of belonging which may accompany being part of a "couple".

At times, when a victim tries to end a relationship, the friends or partner's friends may try to influence the victim to stay in the relationship.

5. LOW SELF-ESTEEM

Victims in violent relationships often question and doubt themselves. They may blame themselves for their partner's behaviors (and the partner reinforces this by telling the victim it is their fault). Experiencing violent and humiliating behavior is likely in itself to lower one's self-esteem.

In long-term relationships and marriages, some additional reasons why victims stay are:

6. ISOLATION

The violent person often criticizes or behaves badly toward the victims's friends and relatives. The abuser may seem to be jealous of any time or attention directed toward others. If the victim finds it too difficult to keep up these relationships, they may find themselves with few friends and little support.

7. FINANCIAL DEPENDENCE

The victim may feel that they cannot support themselves. If the victim has children, she may see that her ability to provide for them without her partner would be at a much lower level. She may have married young and lacks training or skills to earn a living.

8. PERSONAL VALUES

Cultural or family beliefs may place a high value on a relationship or marriage. Fear that divorce or separation will psychologically harm children may encourage a victim to stay in a violent relationship. Victims may hold religious beliefs, which disapprove or forbid ending marriages for any reason.

(Reference: YWCA Family Violence Program-pamphlet)

Chapter Seven

The Abusive Relationship

THE ABUSIVE RELATIONSHIP

"Just what is an abusive relationship? How do I know if I am abused?"
"What are the forms this abuse takes?"

Family violence, domestic violence, or spousal abuses are all terms used to describe a violent or abusive relationship. In an effort to clarify, or make clear, what abuse is, you can start by dividing it into four major categories:

1) PHYSICAL
2) SEXUAL
3) PROPERTY, and
4) PSYCHOLOGICAL.

Programs and specialists throughout the country who work in this area accept this breakdown.

Physical violence or abuse is defined as the use of physical force to intimidate, control, or force another person to do something (or to stop doing something) against his or her will. This includes; grabbing; pushing; holding; slapping; choking; punching; hitting or standing on, kicking; biting, hitting with objects; and assaults with knives, guns, bats, or other weapons or objects.

Sexual violence is the force of another person to engage in any sexual activity through the use of intimidation and the explicit or implicit threat of violence if one's advances or refused.

Property violence usually occurs in a fit of rage and/or as a means to a scare or intimidate. It includes breaking of property, having fits of pounding on the table, putting a fist or foot through a wall or door,

throwing food or other objects, breaking dishes, or any violent behavior using property or objects to intimidate or get your way.
(Usually something with substantial value or sometimes cruelty to pets.)

Psychological violence is usually the most under emphasized of the violent or abusive behaviors, and yet, in some respects the most damaging to the individual because it attacks, and can destroy, the individual's sense of self worth or self-esteem. There are a number of sub-categories to psychological violence.

1. *Explicit threats of violence, such as,"If you don't shut-up, I'm going to slap you."*

2. *Implicit threats of violence, such as; "If you don't stop I don't know what I'm going to do." This is usually accompanied by aggressive behavior such as making a face or "getting in their face."*

3. *Controlling behavior, such as always picking them up at work, dropping them off at school, telling them when they can go out or when they have stay at home, telling them how much they can spend or controlling all the finances yourself, telling them what they can wear, asking them ask for everything, or not allowing them to make individual decisions. Essentially, controlling their whereabouts, companions, and life's activities inside and outside the home.*

4. *Pathological jealousy or looking on others as a threat to the relationship through an illogical fear of losing the other person. This can be a fear of the opposite sex or intense dislike of time spent with family, friends, or even times spent on the job. The behavior that often goes along with this type jealousy frequently includes; accusations of infidelity; confrontations and threats made to the suspected or potential rival; secretive attempts to uncover evidence of infidelity such as following, checking odometer readings,*

questioning friends, frequent telephone calls trying to "catch" them, asking friends to check up or patterns of questions such as "who's that?","Where did you meet them?" "Who was on the phone?" "Where were you?", What did you do? The motivation behind these activities is always to control, intimidate, or occupy the other person in such a way as to eliminate the possibility of losing that person.

5. *Frequent mental degradation in the form of name calling, put downs, criticism, or another method used to make the person receiving this degradation feel bad about themselves.*

6. *Isolating behavior places strict limitations on who your partner can see and when they can see them. This behavior is often rooted in the individual dependence, jealousy, and fear that others will find out about their problems. Isolation from friends and family is often excused by stating that you don't get along with them, you don't like them, they are troublemakers, or they are no good for your partner. This is often done slowly over a period of time and frequently stated in terms designed to show your partner that "it's in their best interest" or "to protect them."*

Abusers who use this category of violence usually are isolated themselves and frequently describe themselves as "loners" or state that "We don't need anybody outside our family."

(Reference: YWCA Family Violence Program)

Chapter Eight

Statistics on Family Violence

Statistics on Family Violence

✓ *There are an estimated five million women battered each year by their husbands, boyfriends or partners.*

✓ *One in four couples will experience some form of violence in their relationship.*

✓ *Of female homicide victims, 30% are killed by their husbands or boyfriends; Of all suicide attempts by women, 25% are a result of abuse.*

✓ *Of visits by women to emergency medical services, 30% are caused by battering.*

✓ *FBI statistics reveal that a woman is beaten every 15 seconds by her husband or partner.*

✓ *Children growing up in abusive homes suffer adverse effects from the abusive environment.*

✓ *Children who witness violence in the home often grow-up to repeat it.*

✓ *A battering incident rarely occurs only once; battering tends to happen repeatedly and become worse over time.*

✓ *Emotional and verbal abuse can be as damaging as physical abuse. Psychological humiliation and isolation are cited by battered women as their worst experiences.*

**Reference: YMCA Family Violence Program*

Chapter Nine

Sophie's Story

"Diary of Trapped Within"
Sophie's Story

Day 1-Thursday-February 29, 1996

Today must be one of the worst days of my life. Today is the first day in traveling down the longest, most lonesome road to healing from Depression for Sophie, my dearest friend on earth.

Unlike my first step in codependent collapse, Sophie's depression is approximately 30 years old and goes on. Her mind has convinced her body to surrender and give up the battle that tried to cover up the sins of others. Sophie, one of the strongest people I have ever known, has endured a lifetime of hurt. Let me review her past.

1) At the age of 2 years old, her natural father left to go to the store one day and never returned. This happened in the days of the Depression and times were very difficult. She must have been totally devastated. She was Rejected.

2) During her childhood and because of her dad's sudden disap-pearance, her brother, and her mother, were forced to live with her grandmother and uncle. The uncle was a drunkard, violent, cursing, hell-trained man. Many times Sophie told me she would stay in a cold, dark room to escape from him.

3) She married a man early in her life who only lived with her for a few months. She told me she really loved him and thought he loved her as well. He, too, was a controller, and lived with his mother. She soon was abandoned by this man and told that she was never loved. She was rejected again.

4) *After the divorce, Sophie went on to marry another man who was a controller. Probably worse, she told me, than any before. Never having the freedoms she deserved she was trapped again.*

5) *Sophie's second husband had an affair that lasted for years with another woman. She knew her, she worked for her, and she despised her. No secrets did this other woman keep from her. Sophie was ordered around in the restaurant like her slave. Sophie's husband and the other woman would insist on going out to eat with Sophie and the other husband. There was a time when Sophie's daughter Anne had an accident and laid near death. George, her husband, did not even tell her about it because he was in a nearby town talking to the other woman. George knew the story, but, did not tell Sophie. Anne almost died that night. Sophie was Rejected again.*

6) *Sophie was completely denied her birthright. All the property her mother and brother owned was taken away from her because of her marriage. This was the punishment she was told she would receive if she married and left the family. Any time moneys were made from the soil of this land, Sophie was not given a dime. Sophie was denied her birthright. She was Rejected again.*

7) *Sophie's mother died in 1993. She was denied the freedom to decide her own mother's funeral arrangements by another family member. She would not allow herself the freedom to mourn because she was trying to please others. This member told her not to cry because it would be a sign of weakness. Sophie could not even mourn the loss of her mother. She was Rejected and controlled again.*

8) *Sophie's children went through difficult divorces. She was pulled through all the divorces, the hurt, and eventually lost five of her grandchildren because of the dispute. Until this day, Sophie still has not seen those grandchildren. All of these facts, in multiplied fashion, tied with the bow of aging of 71 years brought her to this point.*

We had been very concerned over her failing health, and loss of memory. We watched her very closely on Christmas Day, 1995 and saw the inability she had to concentrate and function normally.

On Friday, December 28, 1995, we convinced her to see her doctor about her memory loss. Though Sophie was very embarrassed, she reluctantly told him of her problem with her memory. We felt certain this was a symptom of depression.

After the doctor had examined her and given her several mental tests, he diagnosed her with depression. After reviewing her chart, he told us he had diagnosed this same problem approximately one year before and we did not know it. She never told us of the medication he prescribed for her to take. We calculated this depression back to the time Sophie's entered probably the last and most painful of all events.

The doctor prescribed an anti-depressant, the same as before, and a blood pressure medicine that day. Sophie was given her medicine for approximately three weeks until one of Sophie's relatives told George to stop giving it to her. Foolishly, he took the advice and discontinued Sophie's medicine. During those three weeks of taking medication, Sophie's memory cleared, her speech was no longer distorted, and she seemed to be almost normal again. When the medicine was stopped, she started on the decline, and we watched it. Finally, she started staying in a pitch, dark room 24 hours a day. Sleep and the dark room was the only escape to comfort she could find. She would not eat and never totally rested as she should have. We had to come to this day! We had to do something for Sophie or watch her die!

We had originally planed to take her to a larger hospital in a nearby city today for medical testing. A friend called me and recommended highly to me a new geriatrics unit just recently opened in our town.

We felt it would be better on George if Sophie's hospital could be closer. George would not have to travel so far to see her. This is the place this event is happening.

Molly and I met early this morning at a small restaurant. We were to meet and go together with Sophie to the hospital. When Sophie arrive, she was in a "zombie" state. "Tunnel-vision" had set in—there was no conversation at all—only a cold, dead stare into a world in which she did not want to live. Her little frail body that had lost nearly 15 pounds and was so weak we had to carry her. We took her to the geriatrics unit having to hold her up as she walked. We went inside. It was explained in detail about the unit and the recovery program offered. The Director of Nurses evaluated Sophie and determined she should be confined. She was admitted for depression, possible Alzheimer's disease, and malnutrition. Sophie chose to stay only after we insisted. She knew she was out of time to handle it alone.

We were handed a list of rules to be enforced by the hospital. We were pleased and felt this was the place Sophie should be. We were told she would be tested to eliminate possible medical problems, then chemically tested for proper medications that had been given for depression. Psychological testing would follow to determine depression or possible Alzheimer's disease.

Day 2—Friday-March 1, 1996

Sophie's testing started with blood work, EKG, X-Rays, etc. She was feeling a little flustered and her face expressed it. She did not like the fact she was all-alone, but she refused to leave her bed. Our doctor told us this was her "nest", her "place of safety", where no one could hurt her anymore. She would nestle in her bed and pull the covers up to her head. Several times that day, she closed the blinds to make the room dark. She ate very little today. She asked to see her brother.

We plan to call him to tell him about Sophie.

Day 3—Saturday-March 2, 1996

We had decided to go clean Sophie's house this morning. The house was a disaster. Clothes were everywhere-mixed clean and dirty. My job was the refrigerator. Molly's job was the bathroom. It was apparent, Sophie had been sick a very long time. We found margarine on a plate in the pantry and jelly that was probably years old and molded in the refrigerator. We did our best to reorganize so she would not see the degree her sickness when she was released to come home. When we visited her, she seemed to be resting better, not leaving her nest though, but resting better.

Day 4—Sunday-March 3, 1996

Molly and I went to visit Sophie today. She has no anti-depressants working within her and we could tell. Her memory was probably now at its' worst condition. She was complaining of a headache and wanting to stay in her "bed" (nest) all day. She asked her husband, George, to leave her alone so she could rest. Visiting hours would not be over until 8:00 p.m. It was only 7:00 p.m. I feel she wanted to escape his presence and the pain within. George was an only a reminder of the past she so wanted desperately to escape.

Day 5—Monday-March 4, 1996

More blood-work tests followed today to check the condition of the thyroid. The D.O.N. told me possibly the thyroid balance was low and this could be causing the weakness. Somehow we are hoping this is the medical problem which had added to the depression. If so, we could have answers to our questions. Sophie was very frustrated over being in this place. She was behind locked doors, her visitors were restricted, and very, strict visiting hours only added to the frustration.

As soon as George came into the room, she reprimanded him because he was late(according to Sophie.) Actually George was on time, even five minutes earlier than expected. Sophie accused him of being with his girlfriend. "Sound familiar? Is this proof of what is inside?"

Later that day, she talked to Molly about his affair. The embarrassment and pain she felt was devastating. This had been a forbidden subject for nearly 30 years. We feel this was a great improvement because she wanted to talk about it.

Day 6—Tuesday, March 5, 1996

Today Sophie is eating better and commenting on the good food. The nurses recorded 75% of her food was eaten at mealtime. She says she is feeling more rested. She went to group therapy today but left after about five minutes. Her memory is still so scattered. The doctors and nurses are now beginning to talk more of Alzheimer disease.

"We just will not accept these statements. We know God is healing our Sophie."

Day 7—Wednesday-March 6, 1996

Sophie continues to improve. Though her memory is still at loss and is repeating itself, she has improved in eating. She is also walking down the halls of the unit. Sometimes she will allow the blinds to be opened. She actually made up her bed today, for the first time in months. Today she went to crafts and made a purple flower. This is the first time she has used her hands to create in years. It breaks our hearts to see Sophie being treated as a child. We do realize she must start all over in learning to use her mind and hands. She must also learn to enjoy simple things again.

Day 8—Thursday-March 7, 1996

Today Sophie had several visitors. The nurse told us she was very confused. In her state of depression, she could only comprehend a few words at a time being spoken. If too many visitors were in the room, and she did not understand, she would try to create a conversation using only one word to spare the embarrassment of not knowing what was said. The staff of nurses had asked for visitors to be limited and had restricted George's phone calls. Though George contributed to this cause of her sickness, she,at this point, is still so dependent on him and insists on seeing him. This is a most difficult situation. George is definitely the problem, and Sophie depends on the problem.

Day 9—Friday-March 8, 1996

This morning Molly received a call from the nurses station telling her they had to put Sophie to sleep because she was so angry and frustrated. The nurse had told her she had come to them asking about a car accident. They said she had imagined that one of her family members had been killed. This event was so painful. She was so angry that no one had told her about it. Instantly, I was reminded of the accident her daughter had many years ago and George did not tell her about it until much later. Molly and I was infuriated at the fact she had finally wanted to talk and the staff at the unit gave her medicine to put her to sleep. After repeated happenings such as this, we made plans to find another facility that was, possibly, more qualified to treat this problem. We met with Sophie's doctor and explained how we felt and our plans.

Sophie had been a life long friend. We had made a commitment to her to take care of her as long as we could. He told us our options: 1) to be transferred to another facility or;2) to go home. To be transferred to another facility would mean that Sophie would have to go through another trauma of a new environment, which could be even more damaging to her mental state. To go home prematurely could mean permanent damage to her mental state. He also told us he did not understand why the unit was not working more carefully with her. He also told us he would find out more about it. We went to the unit at 4:30 p.m. to check on Sophie again. We went into her room.

She looked happy and content. She looked rested and her memory was clear. She said the day had been so short. She also told Molly she had cried that morning but it had felt so good. Molly asked her why she cried- whether it was for happy, sad, or mad feelings. Sophie said she was sad. We went with Sophie to eat her dinner. While we were there, the D.O.N. asked to speak with all of us while Sophie was eating. She told us the doctor had spoken to her and told her that we were very frustrated. She wanted to help. She explained to us that Sophie had been very involved in group therapy that morning. She became upset and had to have one-on-one counseling. This created such turmoil within her that she had to be sedated. My argument was, "Is there no one here to give her professional care? Is there no one here to counsel her with the problems she has finally released?" Not only did we have to contend with Sophie fighting to keep her sanity; we had to contend with poor management and incompetent people. We expected experienced professionals to work with this Sophie's depression and we demanded answers.

Day 10—Saturday-March 9, 1996

This morning I went to see Sophie. She really looked bad and was very quiet. There was no smile on her face, not much conversation. When George came in the room she looked the other way. I cannot help but think she had released some pain of the affair and there were no healing words to help her. It was almost as if she was not even in the room. I must believe she will be healed. I remind myself:

Reference—King James
Hebrews 13:8 "Jesus Christ the same yesterday, and to day, and for ever."

Today she was very concerned about her little dog and her cats at home. Big tears came in her eyes when she told me,"I want to go home and see my babies." Sophie has always been an animal lover. She is very sad that she cannot be with them. I fear if she is not allowed to go home soon while her healing is new and fresh, she may start on the down side.

Day 11—Sunday,-March 10, 1996

We went to see Sophie today. She looked somewhat better and her memory was very good. Her anti-depressant was increased this morning. She was very quiet and still. It was said by a very close friend to me, that in situations such as this, one must either flee or fight. Sophie chose to do neither. In my opinion, Sophie self destructed.

Day 12—Monday-March 12, 1996

Today we visited our friend, Sophie. Though she seemed still and quiet, we had noticed the repetitive twitch was gone from her lips that had told us for a very long time of her nervous condition. Later this evening, she expressed to us her desire to go home to see her beloved dog. This dog had been her only companion on which depended for years. Love without demands, without reminders of the past, without fear of being hurt. Just pure, simple love. After years of watching and loving animals, it is my conviction that God has given animals to us for that reason. Animals always love us. They will always stand beside us and love us not matter what we have done in our past. Animals are most theraputical, in my opinion. In this case, "Spot" was Sophie's only true friend on earth. She knew her dog would not ever let her down. We have realized at this point that Sophie must go home soon.

Day 13—Tuesday-March 13, 1996

Today, Sophie seems so much better. Though very cool to George it seems she has received an added confidence and desire to recover— just what we have been praying for. I talked to Molly about Sophie's leaving the unit. We are in agreement, the time is now. We feel if she stays, against her will, she could start on the decline. The doctor and director of the unit are insisting she be transferred and treated for Alzheimer disease. I know the symptoms of Depression and I have seen for myself the destruction of Alzheimer disease. Sophie did not have Alzheimer disease. Sophie had been in severe depression, as first told to us by the Holy Spirit, and, confirmed by the doctor. Never will we receive words of Alzheimer disease on Sophie.

Day 14—Wednesday, March 14, 1996

No way to communicate to the Director of Nurses. She insists on keeping Sophie even though she is better than she has been in years. The doctor of the unit is discussing a transfer of Sophie to another state hospital. We must depend on God to open the doors for her to leave this unit.

Day 15—Thursday, March 15, 1996

Today Molly and I fasted for God to send angels to open the doors and allow Sophie to leave. Sophie's husband, George, does not feel she needs to leave, or the rest of her family. We cannot believe their lack of faith and sight in her recovery. We are convinced Sophie is in the healing process. We cannot talk to the D.O.N. She will not accept our calls. The medical doctor will not accept our calls. In the physical, we had truly realized we had done all we could do to get Sophie released; however, we know God has heard our prayers so we just started praising God for her release.

Day 16—Friday, March 16, 1996

Mysteriously, unexplained without any explanation to the nurses in the unit or to the world, the doctor picked up his pen and wrote Sophie's release today. Only a few hours prior, the doctor had called the state hospital for a transfer for Sophie. Sophie left for home and to see her dog and cats at 10:00 a.m. PRAISE GOD! Sophie has started her healing process—, and she wants to live again.

CLOSING THOUGHTS

I am convinced Sophie came through the program a stronger person within herself and to others. She possibly gained an advantage by looking within herself to see what caused her pain all these years.

The continuation of the healing will be left up to her. Hopefully, she has the strength to cope with George and his unending controlling ways. Combined with medication, to help her body until her total healing arrives, we believe God for recovery! I thank God for doctors and nurses. I respect and appreciate each one of them. Don't be afraid to seek medical help.

I know God and I know He still heals, so seek Him too! Don't ever be afraid to ask someone to help you pray! Don't ever be afraid to listen to your own body. Your body is the temple of the Holy Spirit——

Reference: King James
1 Corinthians 3:16 Know ye not that ye are the temple of God, and that the Spirit of God dwelleth in you?

God expects us to do temple maintenance daily, just as we maintain our earthly dwelling places. God is able! Though this case is quite unusual and yours may not be this severe, the pain is the same. The origin of problem is codependency and the recovery from the injury depends on the determination to overcome.

God opens up the prison doors to those who are bound!

(Reference: King James Isaiah 61:1 "The Spirit of the Lord God is upon me; because the Lord hath anointed me to preach good tidings unto the meek; he hath sent me to bind up the broken hearted, to proclaim liberty to the captives, and the opening of the prison to them that are bound;")

God made a way for our escape!

—(Reference: King James 1 Corinthians 10:13 "There hath no temptation taken you but such as is common to man: but God is faithful, who will not suffer you to be tempted above that ye are able; but will with the temptation also make a way to escape, that ye may be able to bear it.")
By His stripes we are healed!

(Reference—King James Isaiah 53:5 "But he was wounded for our transgressions, he was bruised for our iniquities: the chastisement of our peace was upon him; and with his stripes we are healed.")

Just Believe the Word of God!

Chapter Ten

Annie's Story

—*King James*

Psalms 103:17
But the mercy of the Lord
is from everlasting to everlasting
upon them that fear him,
and his righteousness unto children's
children;

Psalms 103:18
To such as keep his covenant, and to
those that remember his command-
ments to do them.

"ANNIE'S STORY"

I want to tell you before you begin to read this story, the facts of this story are painful and contents are astounding. I ask you to pray that God will enlighten your understanding of the reality of this true story.

This story is about Annie who was a Christian. Witnessing about the love of Jesus to everyone in her daily life was normal. No one found it strange that her discussion was...of Jesus, her best friend. When I say He was her best friend, He was her best friend. Annie loved Jesus, and Jesus loved Annie.

Annie married at 16 years old to Tom, a man who was the oldest son of the family. Because he was the oldest son, he, naturally, was the one receiving the most attention, and probably the most demanding of all children. When Annie married, she like all codependents, gave up her own identity. She surrendered herself to her husband, heart and soul. Annie had watched her mother before her be servant to her father. I remember watching her when I was a child as he would curse her repeatedly in front of our family. Sometimes Tom would push her caus-ing her to stumble, to display his power and control over her before his mother and sisters. I remember Annie crying because he had brought his girlfriend to meet her as if this was an accomplishment. I was once told that Tom would not keep secrets of his love life from Annie. He had somehow convinced Annie that it was all right for his girlfriend to come over to visit at their house. I remember his drunkenness.

One night when I was seven years old, we went to a party he was having on his new boat. He had bought himself a new boat to display his successfulness. He was generous though; he named it the "Miss Annie." I begged my mother and dad not to go, but my dad insisted on going. Because there was no one to baby-sit me, I was had no choice but to tag along. The night was cool and damp. The boat was very small. I remember well, Tom was so drunk he stumbled through the narrow halls of the boat.

Annie was trying to cook french fries on a too small stove. I wondered if hot grease was going to burn mother, Annie, or me when one of us stumbled into it. I was standing beside my mom and he almost knocked the hot skillet of grease over on me as he walked by. He cursed violently and jerked Annie by her arm. Annie only apologized for him and tried to get away from him. Tom grabbed her up, started kissing on her, and then dragged her to the sofa where started to make his sexual advances. I, a child, was horrified. I closed my eyes tightly because I was so afraid. All I could think was here we were, out in the middle of the lake. I felt as though it was only Annie, my Mom and me, and the unknown of a new boat. This was the fear inside of a seven-year-old child. I started to cry because I was so afraid. With so much hate in his voice, he told me to, "shut up—I ain't listening to no squalling kid— why didn't ya'll leave her at home."In trying not to cry-caused me to sob vehemently-all the louder. This infuriated Tom and he glared at me with eyes of fire. I held tightly to my Mom. I thought the night would never be over.

There was another occasion when Annie and Tom's daughter wanted me to stay overnight with them. At about 2:00 a.m. I heard a terrible crash. The crash came from Tom throwing a vase at Annie because he was drunk again. He was going throughout the house screaming obscenities and cursing. Occasionally, he would hit the walls with his fists. Annie's cries echoed through the house as she pleaded with him to give up his alcohol and women. I hear her cries today in my mind.

Tom was a handsome man and all women went after him. Tom loved women. He never kept secret from Annie of his many loves, always apologized for his affairs, and promised her he would never go out on her again. If Annie complained of the past or pleaded with him to come home on time, he cursed her and dared her to complain. Yet, Annie loved Tom. Annie thought she could not live without him. She forgave him when he never asks her to.

Annie had two children for Tom. When Tom got older, his health began to fail him and his doctor told the family he could have no more surgeries. Annie was horrified. She felt responsible somehow that she could never make him happy enough. Annie felt fully responsible for Tom's health problems and promised him she would always be there to take care of him.

Once again, humbled by his condition, she resigned herself to taking care of Tom. Tom would not allow Annie to shop because it would use too much gasoline to get to the local mall, which was approximately five miles from their house. He said the mall was too far away. He did not want the extra miles on his car, but, if she would pay for the gas then he would take her. Annie never received any money for anything from Tom. Even groceries were monitored, common routine trips to the grocery store were denied to Annie. Two children grew up in this environment that could make hell seem like a playhouse. Annie's entire life was made up of these stories. Tom was never at fault in the eyes of his family. Annie was always trying to please. Annie's entire life with Tom was filled with events such as this. Annie probably never knew who she was or what exactly her purpose was in this life. I am sure what I have told you has drawn an awful feeling of nausea in your stomach but—imagine Annie. Annie lived in this environment 24 hours a day-7 days a week.

Early one morning a few days ago, I received a call that Annie had gone to be with Jesus. Annie had awakened at approximately 3:30 a.m. that morning with her chest hurting. She complained of feeling smothered. When Annie arrived at the hospital, the doctor's diagnosed her as having a massive heartattack. Annie left this world at approximately 6:30 a.m. that day. I was so hurt and I was in such disbelief that such a Christian witness could have been taken. I cried, then I cried some more.

In the scripture, God tells us,

—Reference King James
James 1:5 If any of you lack wisdom, let him ask of God,
that giveth to all men liberally, and upbraideth not; and it
shall be given him.

So I did. I began to talk to God and ask him why Annie had been taken. "Why, Lord, why Annie? She was such a witness for you...Why?"
In the sweetest voice I have ever heard, God spoke to my spirit and said, "Annie is free. I have broken the chains from her feet. I promised her I would not place more on her than she could bear and I didn't. Annie is free."

Reference King James:
—King James
1 Corinthians 10:13 "There hath no temptation taken you
but such as is common to man: but God is faithful, who
will not suffer you to be tempted above that ye are able; but
will with the temptation also make a way to escape, that ye
may be able to bear it."

When God placed this truth in my spirit, the Holy Spirit caused me to remember and the understanding came to me. Many times in all Tom's raging fits, Annie would call us and ask us to help her pray. Many times she told us she had prayed, "Lord, I just can't take anymore." After repeated times of listening to Annie's request and feeling her pain we feel,

God finally said, "That's it...,no more.
My child will not hurt anymore."

I started to rejoice in knowing Annie was with God. I rejoiced in knowing God will rescue us. I rejoiced in having the full knowledge that God would make a way for our escape.

God will not let us hurt more than we can stand. I rejoiced in knowing Annie was with him, free from the chains of codependency a subject she knew nothing about but lived it to the fullest. It is my understanding now that God could not stand to see her hurt and abused any longer.

Jesus paid the price for our peace!

Reference—King James
Isaiah 53:5 But he was wounded for our transgressions, he was bruised for our iniquities: the chastisement of our peace was upon him; and with his stripes we are healed.

God made a way for her escape as He promised in His Word!

This truth made a drastic difference in how I felt about Annie's passing. It's no longer "poor Annie", as she had been called in years past because of Tom's abuse to her. It is now "poor us" left here for awhile longer living without Annie. A friend of mine was given the vision of Jesus placing a crown on Annie's head.

Annie looked into His eyes, took the crown from her head and placed it at His feet. Annie's life was such an inspiration to me. The way she loved God, and her dramatic story, helped in my recovery from codependency.

*The following Sunday I was in our praise service at church. As the band played, people praised and worshiped to the tune of "**Victory in Jesus**." This was always one of Annie's favorite songs and the praise leader had no way of knowing this. The verse that says,*

**"I heard about a mansion he has built for me in glory,
I heard about those streets of gold,
beyond the crystal sea..."**

In a vision, I saw Annie standing in front of me nodding her head saying, "Yes, it's here, yes, it's here."

God was so precious to comfort my heart in such a dynamic way. Such power, such love, God has for us, to protect us at any cost. He will remove us from his witnessing field to carry us to HIS presence. I did not know His grace and love extended to this degree, probably should have, but didn't! There is such peace in knowing he will rescue us.

I miss Annie but I know that someday I will see her again!

-King James
John 14:2 In my Father's house are many mansions: if it were not so, I would have told you. I go to prepare a place for you.

-King James
John 14:3 And if I go and prepare a place for you, I will come again, and receive you unto myself; that where I am, there ye may be also.

Chapter Eleven

Codependency and the Christian

CODEPENDENCY and the CHRISTIAN

Codependents have many traits. We are caretakers. I know you are probably saying by now, Christians are called to be caretakers. Yes, we are, but; we must remember in being caretakers, we must not forget to care for ourselves first. We must know the boundaries of taking care of others. We must know how far to go in caring and when to let go.

Codependents...love too much. Again, we as Christians are commanded to love but; we must love ourselves first as Jesus commanded us in;

Reference—King James
Matthew 19:19 "Honour thy father and thy mother: and,
Thou shalt love thy neighbour as thyself."

"Love thy neighbor as thyself."

As thyself—first we must love ourselves, then we can truly love others. Loving others comes so easy for the Christian following Jesus. It is most easy to forget about ourselves. We get wrapped up in the pain of others and lose our joy, thus, causing us to lose our strength. We must be very cautious in this area of recovery. Codependents try to fix things beyond our control. We must beware of the boundaries of repair. Only God can 'fix' things.

When people we love have problems, or situations to which they call on us for help, we must really get down and ask ourselves, "Will I really be helping them with this problem, or, causing the problem to be greater by interfering?"

"Will I create a situation worse than it would have been if I stay out of it?" We must remember to let go and let God. We must remember to pray, then let go of the problem, and let God.

Reference—King James
1 Peter 5:7 "Casting all your care upon him; for he careth for you."

If God needs us to help Him, I assure you He knows how to arrange it all to happen. You must remember it was our God who spoke stars into space and all of them were spoken perfectly. God spoke all creation into place and it was perfect.

Reference:—King James
Genesis 1:1 "In the beginning God created the heaven and the earth."

God can repair the problems and is quick to hear the cries off His children!

—King James
1 Peter 3:12 For the eyes of the Lord are over the righteous, and his ears are open unto their prayers: but the face of the Lord is against them that do evil.

The very best thing we can do for others having problems is to keep a constant, on line relationship with God. When we feel we are in too deep, ask God to help. Codependents offer help to others when we really don't want to. Because we do not have the courage to "say no", we create a more difficult situation for ourselves and for others, too.

Codependents will subconsciously plan a way of escape for ourselves if things get too rough. When the pain of mental abuse or physical abuse becomes greater than we can stand, the escape plan becomes evident.

We find ourselves subconsciously looking for a way out and we will find it, such as was my story. I have been a Christian for 42 years and I thought something this terrible could not happen to me. He made a way for an escape from my inferiority complex and the spirits of rejection. These roots were deep and had grown into a stronghold on my life. Praise God! Strongholds can be broken through God's power.

Reference-King James
2 Corinthians 10:4 "For the weapons of our warfare are not carnal, but mighty through God to the pulling down of strong holds;"

Strongholds were broken from my life by God's power!

I know many of you have experienced similar mental abuse stories beginning in your childhood and probably carried over into your marriage. Some of you have not yet escaped-because you are not aware there is a way out; or, you have been so brutally abused that you feel you are not worthy of a better life. Some of you have resigned yourself to live in a state of abuse whether mental or physical. I want to tell you that you do not have to stay in that place. God has a healing power for you. He has the Master Plan for your life. You are special to Him. He has given to you traits and talents only for you. Everything about you is special and beautiful because God is perfect and all things created by Him are perfect. We were chosen before the foundations of the world and He has known us since that time.

Reference: King James
Ephesians 1:4 "According as he hath chosen us in him
before the foundation of the world, that we should be holy
and without blame before him in love:

Reference—King James
Ephesians 1:5 "Having predestinated us unto the adoption
of children by Jesus Christ to himself, according to the
good pleasure of his will,"

Reference:—King James
Ephesians 1:6 "To the praise of the glory of his grace,
wherein he hath made us accepted in the beloved."

God loves you and has a divine purpose for you in His
work!

Chapter Twelve

The Anchor Holds

THE ANCHOR HOLDS

As far back as I can remember, I was taken to a little denominational church three times a week. I would dress up with my "stand out" slip on, (a term from my generation) my frilly dresses and my black patent shoes. No reason kept us from attending any services. My Dad was a deacon of the local church. A straight and structured figure of a man with some respectful ways. I remember the old, white, frame, church-building. Tall steps that invited you in and two big heaters standing on the floor with a blue flame that seemed to reach the ceiling. The sounds of my mother playing the piano echoed loudly across the room. The sounds seemed to bounce with praise from wall to wall. My mother is so gifted with music. God gave her the gift of playing by ear using no written music of any kind. Just a natural talent. How wonderful is the sound!

I attended church services until I married. One of the largest problems I ever encountered in this denomination was over the design of the new building. It seemed some of the people thought we needed to improve and update our building. Thus, the war started.

"Ceilings eight feet? No...nine feet! Carpet on the floor? No...carpet on the floor. Padded pews? No padded pews." The warfare was tremendous, so much that it divided the fellowship. As I stated, my Dad was a deacon and remember...a controller. He was so fixed on his opinion being the only one, and the right one, it seemed he could not hear anyone else. He was determined to have his way, and, this building be built according to his specifications. He talked with the others, he maneuvered as controllers will do, but the people continued to go in the other direction. Finally, one day, he realized he no longer could

persuade the decision, so, he just decided he would not go to church anymore. He, also, forbid my mom and I to go. Since he could not control the construction of the new building program, he **could** control, his family, and our attendance to it. (If you remember, we had no opinion, we had no choice in this situation.)

For a few months, my mom and I visited other churches. He allowed us to go to church services, just not the one to which he was in disagreement. For many years, we went by ourselves-just Mom and me.

We went from one denominational church to another trying to find that missing link we both knew we needed. Jesus found me when I was seven years old. At the tender age of seven, I was in love with Jesus! Both then, and now, I am in love with him! I was baptized in a community pond. I remember very well wading out, into the water, and the mud squashing between my toes. I remember the water covering my face as I went beneath it and the feeling of renewal when I arose. I felt so clean, and so ready for heaven, even at seven years old! I knew for a long time there was more, and soon I was not content to go to a denomination that ignored the chapters of Psalms, which told of all the music in praise to the Lord. Then...there was the book of Acts-of the filling of the Holy Spirit! There was no denying that part of the Word, because it is written. I saw this as a child. Every church service we attended had the same denominational teaching, but none had the power I knew was written in the Word of God. In my spirit, I knew I was destined to have all of God! The power of the Holy Spirit was never taught to me in my childhood, but He knew me, and had a grip on my heart. The Holy Spirit lived in my Mom, and I saw Him!

When I married at seventeen, I had a deep hunger for more of the Lord. I knew there was more of his love and a deeper walk, but , had no idea of how or where to find it. At 35 years old, I was baptized again— still in love with Jesus. I never doubted my salvation. I wanted to be like Jesus. I wanted to experience again what I felt as a child being baptized. I sincerely wanted to follow Jesus and still do! Shortly after, I was *called to work in a children's ministry for the local denominational church. We worked so carefully with those children, taught them of praise and worship inside this denominational church . We taught these children the real love of Jesus and how He taught us to live. Being a denominational church, this teaching was quite different. It seemed, as though, some just can not understand my radical love I have for Jesus. I soon left that fellowship because of spiritual differences of opinion. When I left I was in peace with the Holy Spirit, for I knew if the Holy Spirit was not welcome in that place, then I was not either!*

*Soon after, I found another denominational church that **did** have praise and worship, such as I had never known. However, it was bound by denominational teaching with its own rules and laws established, by man, omitting some of the writings of the Word.*

*I just did not enjoy the fact that some man or woman was sitting in authority mandating people to teach **only** what they wanted them to know. Again, my search for peace soon carried me away and I moved on—in search for a service—where the Word was taught in truth, no omissions, no man-made teachings, just Jesus and His Holy Spirit. I insisted on finding the truth! I searched and searched; and I prayed and prayed. While I searched, I was constantly reminded in the Word of the woman at the well and how Jesus told her to worship in Spirit and truth.*

Reference-King James
John 4:20 "Our fathers worshipped in this mountain; and ye say, that in Jerusalem is the place where men ought to worship."

Reference—King James
John 4:21 "Jesus saith unto her, Woman, believe me, the hour cometh, when ye shall neither in this mountain, nor yet at Jerusalem, worship the Father."

Reference—King James
John 4:23 "But the hour cometh, and now is, when the
true worshippers shall worship the Father in <u>spirit and in</u>
<u>truth</u>: for the Father seeketh such to worship him."

I would get so excited. I knew in my heart someday I would find Him in all His truth and praise.

The Word tells us in:

Reference—King James
2 Corinthians 3:17 "Now the Lord is that Spirit: and where
the Spirit of the Lord is, there is liberty."

I locked on to this scripture and held it tightly in my heart!

*At that time, a friend of mine was in the same search for a fellowship just described. She called me one day and told me of a full-gospel fellowship where **the Word was taught in its entirety and the Spirit of the Lord was there.***

This church was approximately 30 miles from us, but, mileage just did not matter. When I walked in that place, I could not believe what I was seeing and hearing! Instruments of every kind and number. Music, praise, liberty, liberty, liberty! The presence and the power of the Lord were so great in the place—I really wondered if the walls were about to fall. It is still awesome. I simply can not wait to get back to each service.

God had delivered me!
God kept His promise!
God brought me here!
Oh! the joy and praise did flood my heart!

*We are still attending this fellowship and it continues to grow and multiply each Sunday as did in the early days of Acts. The first churches of Acts grew rapidly. So does ours. We are taught how to live the **abundant life** Jesus promised.*

Reference King James
John 10:10 The thief cometh not, but for to steal, and to kill, and to destroy: I am come that they might have life, and that they might have it more abundantly.

The Holy Spirit is with us continually and I praise God for His presence. For your ultimate spiritual growth and support, I recommend you to go in search for a fellowship as this. If you do, your recovery will be much easier because you will have freedom in the Spirit that is absolutely essential for your codependent recovery.

As I can see, I was appointed to be alone and adrift in order to find my perfect walk with God. God had his eye on my life and had a plan and a path chosen for me.

—King James
Ephesians 1:11 In whom also we have obtained an inheritance, being predestinated according to the purpose of him who worketh all things after the counsel of his own will:

Spiritual lessons of my childhood, though devastating as they were, only strengthened and led me to recover from this abusive bondage. Because my mother—keeping me close to God in my childhood—a foundation was created within me of God's truth-mandatory to survive in the walk of codependent recovery. It took God to break the stronghold of the denomination, and, courage to leave the denominational structure. I did not do this on my own, it was God who gave me strength! I had to have all the Word of God!

I could not settle for only part of it. I chose to walk with God and because I did...my life changed! I had started down the road of recovery and I did not even know I had been codependent! And I am still in Recovery! But...I am daringly different!

God is no respector of persons.

Reference—King James
Acts 10:34 "Then Peter opened his mouth, and said, Of a truth I perceive that God is no respector of persons"

What He has done for me...He WILL do for you!!

Chapter Thirteen

Tell Them About My Stripes

"Tell Them About the Stripes On My Back"

Jesus was brutally whipped and beaten in order that you and I could have a mind to function in peace. Jesus loved us so much that he was beaten, then crucified, died the most horrible death ever recorded, so that we might live forever.

Reference—King James
Isaiah 53:3 "He is despised and rejected of men; a man of sorrows, and acquainted with grief: and we hid as it were our faces from him; he was despised, and we esteemed him not."

In this scripture, Isaiah told us Jesus also paid the price for rejection, as we codependents sometimes feel. The spirit of rejection is one of the most forceful of demonic spirits Hell could send upon us. It seems nothing hurts us as deeply as rejection.

This scripture also describes Jesus as a man of sorrows and acquainted with grief. Codependents are definitely acquainted with grief before we enter our recovery through Jesus. I feel this could have been why Jesus addressed this so clearly, because He knew some of us would be facing rejection, abuse, sorrow, and grief. This is our proof that Jesus paid the price for our healing recovery from codependency. He made a way for us as He promised He would do.

I hope you can see a little more clearly why we can walk freely and be delivered from any forces of control or abuse? In order for you to walk the same road of codependent recovery as I did, with healing that only Jesus can give, it will be mandatory to meet Jesus and begin a personal relationship with Him. You may be wondering by now how you can enter into a personal relationship with Jesus such as I have with Him.

It is very simple!

"Just give your life to Jesus!"

Reference—King James
Romans 10:9 "That if thou shalt confess with thy mouth
the Lord Jesus, and shalt believe in thine heart that God
hath raised him from the dead, thou shalt be saved."

Reference—King James
Romans 10:10 "For with the heart man believeth unto
righteousness; and with the mouth confession is made unto
salvation."

Salvation—Saved—-New Life!

Praise God! You Are Free!

Chapter Fourteen

Know Who You are!

KNOW WHO YOU ARE NOW

One of the first steps in our new life will be to go deep inside our mind to the place where all dreams are stored and created. The old codependent nature allowed people to rob us of our dreams and goals. We have within us a destiny that God has already set in place. We have dreams just waiting to be fulfilled.

—King James
Ephesians 1:5 Having predestinated us unto the adoption of children by Jesus Christ to himself, according to the good pleasure of his will….

—King James
Ephesians 1:6 To the praise of the glory of his grace, wherein he hath made us accepted in the beloved.

When I was a child, on occasion I would go with my grandmother to have her hair styled on Saturday mornings. I watched carefully as the hair stylist so diligently set and combed her hair. From that time, the goal was established to be a licensed Cosmetologist. I love my work because I feel I have been called by God and given the creative talents to perform. God has placed inside of each one of us specialized talents. Each person has a different talent and gift only he or she can give to the world. In order to find these talents, we must be fine-tuned to ourselves in God. We must seek within ourselves our own enjoyment in life. Then, we should choose a place of employment in that field, that we will enjoy what we do! God did not intend for us to be unhappy. God wants us to be happy and to live an abundant life.

God has known you and I before the foundations of the world.

Reference—King James
Ephesians 1:4 "According as he hath chosen us in him
before the foundation of the world, that we should be holy
and without blame before him in love:"

In our old codependent nature we were people pleasers. We tried to please and cater to everyone except ourselves. When something would go wrong, we would try to take the blame in order to protect the best in others. The Codependent will seek approval from everyone. They never give themselves credit for being able to think situations through, and if they should, they will not trust their own judgment. When you think about it, trusting comes from loving someone. That will tell you that codependents must love themselves as Jesus commanded them to. They must truly love that person within, before they can trust the person within with judgments of a situation. Most times codependents spend their entire life catering all their time to others. They forget the simple things that come freely.

One day while my daughters and I were having a "pow—wow" as we often times do, I ask them to name some of their favorite things. Their favorite things consisted of:

driving down the road in the late afternoon after a rain with the windows down,
the sound of a softball hitting against a bat in the late afternoon,
the smell of smoke-leaves burning on a cool day,
the smell of fresh cut grass,
a dog's friendly wagging tail,
a warm flannel shirt on the first day of fall,
a bright, starry sky on a clear night,
a fresh, early, chilly morning with a radiant blue sky which makes you feel you can see forever,

driving down the road with the windows down and your favorite song comes on the radio,

waking up in the middle of the night to the sound of thunder-knowing a storm is coming,

a cat smiling at you,

a cold, wintry day with hot soup on the stove and a slow fire in the fireplace.

These are only a few of our favorite things. I am sure there are millions of others you have in your life if you have ever stopped and noticed.

I heard it once said that the very best things in life are free. When we as codependents have come to the place of total destruction and to the point of what seems to be no return, this is the time we need to focus on the very best things in life that ARE free.

Simple things...such as a gentle rain on a brand new morning! This morning I rode with my husband as he left for work, to the top of the hill, a distance of probably 200 feet, to get the newspaper. A beautiful feeling was in the air. A gentle sprinkle of rain, a slight chill in the air, in the background a few birds supplied the music because they, too, had found the same wonder as I. The sweet smell of the air, all of God's wonder, just for you and me and it cost nothing—just there for our enjoyment!

I feel God specializes in mornings!

I feel He prepares a glorious beginning and gives us the freedom to enjoy or ignore. Why don't you ask yourself a few questions now—

"Did you get too busy in a job today to notice your favorite things?" Then ask God to change this for you.

"Did you allow your job to deprive you of this beautiful morning?" Then ask God to remind you to slow down.

"Did a spouse deprive you of a special moment—because you are so codependent you were trying to make him happy—and did not take the time? And...because his feelings, at this point in your life, are more important than your own? Then ask God to set you free!

"Did you deny yourself that one minute of freedom to enjoy God's prism rainbow bouncing off the window pane?" Then ask God to show you another view.

"Did you just take for granted that beautiful flower that proudly stood displaying the drop of fresh morning dew?" Then ask God to open your eyes.

When you begin to search for YOUR favorite things, you will begin to notice your life has become richer, simpler, and you will appreciate those finer things. You will find more wonderful favorites about yourself you did not know existed. I learned these moments were, and still are, a very large part of my healing recovery and could be part of yours. I try to always make sure I continue to notice God's handiwork. In doing this, I am reminded how awesome He is and how wonderful He is. God is so artistic to give His creation such color and style. How much more does He have for you and I? All of these special times will be such a help for you...and have been there all the time!

Enjoy the Rainbow!

—King James
Genesis 9:13 I do set my bow in the cloud, and it shall be for a token of a covenant between me and the earth.

I encourage you to try relaxing from your busy schedule for just a few minutes, to another place in time to your favorite things...then enjoy...and wait for its return!!

Chapter Fifteen

Dance in Fields of Yellow Daffodils

"DANCE IN FIELDS OF YELLOW DAFFODILS"

One of the sweetest experiences Jesus has ever given to me was a few years ago. This was one of dancing with Him in a field of yellow daffodils!

It happened one afternoon after an awful day at work. I had been harassed by several spirits of control and aggravated by spirits of fear on my job. I was aggravated with me for allowing myself to be harassed. Because of this, I felt I had failed in the way I had handled a certain situation. That night I rested in a time of meditation. I rested and I closed my eyes. I started to think about Jesus and all He has done for me. I started to think about how much He loves me and what He endured for me. I remembered His love and how He told me He would never leave me nor forsake me. He told me He would be with me always, and I knew that would be through the good and the bad! He told me He would be my Counselor and Friend.

As I pondered these thoughts, I was taken in my spirit into a field—a field as far as I could see—of yellow daffodils. The wind was blowing— huge trees lined each side of the field and the tops swayed in the wind. Birds were singing and my soul was at peace. I was in awe at the beauty of the place. As I looked across the field, I saw a man dressed in a long white robe walking toward me. He was so handsome. He was tall, and well groomed. His hair and beard was dark and long.

I instantly recognized this as being Jesus. I ran to Him and as I ran to Him, He stretched His arms to meet me. When I reached Him, He held me for a few minutes then we started to dance. It seemed we waltzed for hours. We laughed and we talked with every turn we made to the angelic music. *His hair was blowing in the wind and the light of His smile did show brightly on my face. My vision soon ended and I was removed from the field of yellow daffodils by the reality of my beautiful children entering the room. The sounds of their voices were those of angels and I paused to thank Him for my three blessings.*

You may not realize the power of this story, but you see, no one in my family knew I loved to dance. No one knew I loved waltzing-not even my husband. But Jesus knows all about me. He knows I love dancing and He meets me in that field of yellow daffodils when I am weary.

I have realized His presence is still with me; and He does just as He promised:

Reference—King James
John 14:18 "I will not leave you comfortless: I will come to you."

Reference—King James
John 14:19 "Yet a little while, and the world seeth me no more; but ye see me: because I live, ye shall live also."

Reference—King James
John 14:20 "At that day ye shall know that I am in my Father, and ye in me, and I in you."

Reference—King James
John 14:27 "Peace I leave with you, my peace I give unto you: not as the world giveth, give I unto you. Let not your heart be troubled, neither let it be afraid."

So you see, my life has changed dramatically. I have come a long way in my recovery process, however; one never arrives. Our walk is daily!

Reference—King James
Luke 9:23 "And he said to them all, If any man will come
after me, let him deny himself, and take up his cross daily,
and follow me."

Each day we should wake up rejoicing in knowing we have Jesus,
whom we can depend on and...our Friend—we will gladly follow!

Jesus , Lover of My Soul!

THE ROAD NOT TAKEN

Two roads diverged in a yellow wood,
And sorry I could not travel both
And be one traveler, long I stood
And looked down one as far as I could
To where it bent in the undergrowth;

Then took the other, as just as fair,
And having perhaps the better claim.
Because it was grassy and wanted wear;
Though as for that the passing there
Had worn them really about the same,

And both that morning equally lay
In leaves no step had trodden black.
Oh, I kept the first for another day!
Yet knowing how way leads on to way,
I doubted if I should ever come back.

I shall be telling this with a sigh
Somewhere ages and ages hence:
Two roads diverged in a wood, and I
I took the one less traveled by,
and that has made all the difference.

Robert Frost

I want to Thank You for allowing me to share with you the steps I have taken down the "road less traveled."
I had a choice:
To travel down the narrow road less traveled of
Healing Recovery or:
To stay on the wide path of destruction in bondage to Controllers.
When I made my choice to follow God down the straight and narrow path to Recovery....
He was there to show me the way!

(I will be praying for you!)

All Scripture quotations, unless indicated, are taken from the Holy Bible, copyrighted 1976 by Thomas Nelson, Inc. 1976. Scripture quotations referenced are taken from the King James Version.

Endnotes:

Part One-Chapter 2-Alone and Adrift-Mary Jones.March.1996
Part Two-Chapter 4-Letter From My Friend-Jan Wheeler.4199 Hwy.452.Marksville.LA.June.1996

References:

Frost, Robert. Collected Poems of Robert Frost. 1930. NY: Á Halcyon House Edition, March, 1939.

"YWCA Family Violence Program". Pamphlet. YWCA of Northwest Louisiana. A United Way Agency. Date Unknown.

The information in this book was
based on

A true story;

However,

Some parts and names could have been
altered for

Publication purposes.

I would like to thank you for investing in your life!

It was not by chance you found this book-I feel it was by God's direction in your life that brought us together. I am interested your progress in the recovery program from codependency you have now started. The first step you made was purchasing and reading this book. You are now on the way. Your life now has new meaning you will need special care while learning to grow.

As part of our Ministry, I would like to follow-up with you, and pray for you daily. Please fill in the below form and mail it back to me so I can continue to help you!!

May God Bless You and Be With You Always!

Mail to: **In the Master's Service Ministries**
           353 CrossRoads Loop-Farmerville, LA 71241

Email:lojnjesus@yahoo.com

Name: _____

Address: _____

           _____

*Telephone No.*_____

FAX No. _____

*Email address:*_____

*Faith Affiliation:*_____

Comments to
*share:*_____

_____

_____

_____

**Please find peace in knowing all information will remain confidential

www.ingramcontent.com/pod-product-compliance
Lightning Source LLC
Chambersburg PA
CBHW031238280526
45784CB00004B/1630